THE PRAIRIES
AND THEIR PEOPLE

David Flint

Thomson Learning
New York

PEOPLE
· AND PLACES ·

The Amazon Rain Forest and its People

The Arctic and its People

The Prairies and their People

The Sahara and its People

First published in the
United States in 1993 by
Thomson Learning
115 Fifth Avenue
New York, NY 10003

First published in 1993 by
Wayland (Publishers) Ltd

Library of Congress Cataloging-in-Publication Data applied for

ISBN 1-56847-154-8

Printed in Italy

Cover: Harvesting a crop of wheat from a prairie field.

Title page: Harvesting soybeans, an important crop on the prairies.

Contents page: Oil refineries, like this one in Canada, are changing the face of the prairies.

Acknowledgments
The publisher would like to thank the following for allowing their photographs to be reproduced in this book: Eye Ubiquitous 35 (L. Johnstone); David Graham 43; Images 36; Impact 4 (Francesca Yorke), 29 (John Cole); Peter Newark's Western Americana 13, 14, 15, 16, 18, 20, 22, 23, 25 (Western-Firo); Photri 7 (Hungerford), 9, 11, 12 (John Grant), 17, 19 (Leonard Lee Rue III), 21, 32, 38, 39 (Andrews-Orange), 42 (Gary Funck), 44; NASA/Science Photo Library 34, Tony Stone 3 (Peter Baumgartner), 28 (Andy Sacks), 41 (Andy Sacks), James Wilson 8; Zefa cover, 26 (Joe Sohm), 27 (Roger du Buisson), 31, 37.
Photo on page 1 comes from the Wayland Picture Library.
Artwork by Peter Bull (5, 18, 24, 33, 40) and Tony Smith (6, 7, 10, 30, 43).

CONTENTS

The prairies of North America were originally a huge area of grassland. They stretched 1,500 miles from north to south, and up to 800 miles from east to west, covering an area of 1.2 million square miles. The prairies occupy the center of the North American continent, lying between the Rocky Mountains in the west and the forests of the east and south. They extend from the Prairie Provinces of Canada in the north to Kansas, Oklahoma, and Texas to the south. The first Native Americans to live there called the area the "tall grasses." Later, some of the first European explorers who reached these grassy plains were from France. The tall grasses reminded them of the meadows in their own country so they called them by their word, "prairies." On their western fringes in the United States, the prairies are called the Great Plains.

◄

In the western part of the prairies, the grasslands are drier and have shorter grass than farther east. They are bordered by the Rocky Mountains.

The prairies lie at the heart of North America.

►

PACIFIC
OCEAN

BRITISH
COLUMBIA   ALBERTA

Edmonton
SASKATCHEWAN

Calgary

WASHINGTON

MONTANA   NORTH
DAKOTA   MINNESOTA   Lake Superior   GREAT
LAKES

IDAHO   SOUTH
DAKOTA   WISCONSIN

WYOMING   NEBRASKA   IOWA   Chicago

Denver   ILLINOIS

COLORADO   KANSAS   MISSOURI

OKLAHOMA   ARKANSAS

NEW
MEXICO

TEXAS

MEXICO   Gulf of Mexico

MANITOBA

ONTARIO

ROCKY MOUNTAINS

0   100   200   300   400   500 mi.

— — — Boundary of prairies

Tallgrass prairies

Short-grass prairies

Grasses: Well Adapted to the Prairies

Grasses have slim, hollow stems and straight, narrow leaves. They are well adapted to survive in the harsh conditions of the prairies.

When it becomes very cold or very dry, the top parts of the grass – the leaves and stem – can die. However, the plant as a whole does not die. The roots remain alive. Then when conditions become warmer and wetter, grasses can grow quickly from their roots by sending up new shoots. The plant can produce flowers and seeds very quickly in the **short growing season. Below the surface, grass roots spread far and wide and new plants also grow from these.** **Their hollow stems allow them to bend but not break in high winds that sweep across the prairies.**

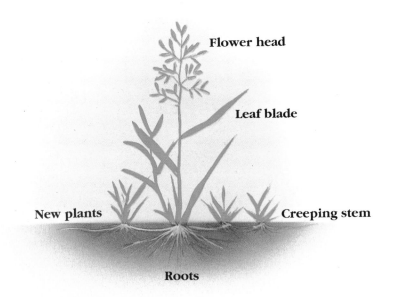

Flower head

Leaf blade

New plants

Creeping stem

Roots

WET AND DRY PRAIRIES

The grasslands vary over the vast area of the prairies. In general, the prairie grass is taller and denser in the wetter east. Moving west, conditions are much dryer, and the prairie grass is shorter.

There are more than 8,000 types of grass in the world, and more than 2,000 of these can be found on the prairies. In the wetter eastern prairies the main types of grass are bluestem grass and Indian grass, which both grow over 6.5 feet high. In some even wetter parts, bottlebrush grass is found.

Conditions throughout the prairies are not wet enough for trees to grow well. In the past there were a few trees, such as oaks and cottonwoods, scattered across the wetter, eastern grasslands, especially along the rivers. However, those trees were cut down for fuel, fencing, or houses for the European settlers. New trees have not been able to establish themselves easily because grazing animals, such as cattle and sheep, have eaten the saplings, and because much of the area has been plowed.

The prairie grasslands are changing all the time. These changes are in response to the effects of people, animals, and fluctuating climate. Grasses eaten by grazing animals, such as buffalo or cattle, grow thicker and stronger each time their shoots are eaten. Periodic fires clear the old grass and allow new shoots to develop. The grasses themselves add organic matter to the soil as well as chemicals that act like antibiotics. These chemicals kill some types of plants, while other flowering plants thrive on them and spread.

The eastern prairies do not consist solely of grasses. They also have orchids such as the white-fringed orchid or the yellow lady's slipper, as well as clover and poppies. This region of the prairies gets about 30 inches of rain or snow each year. The grasses grow well, producing a lot of roots and organic material that make the soil deep, black, and very fertile. In turn, this soil supports many other plants that also provide homes and food for a large number of insects, birds, animals, and reptiles.

▲
Natural prairie land supports a wide variety of grasses and flowering plants.

To the west, conditions are much drier. Here, places near the Rocky Mountains may get less than 12 inches of rain or snow a year. The grass does not grow as tall. Buffalo grass is typical of these drier conditions,

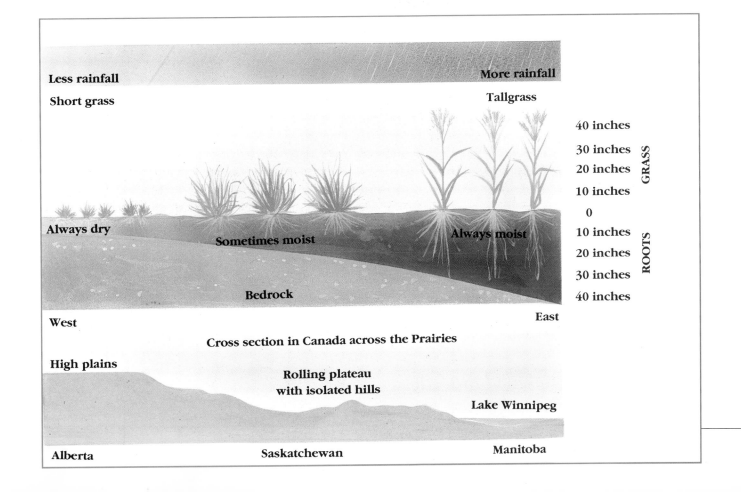

growing to a height of two feet or less. As a result there are fewer roots and less organic material in the soil, making it shallower and light brown. In the much drier, semi-arid parts of the west, bare rock and soil may even be exposed between clumps of spindly grass or sagebrush. There is not enough moisture to support many grasses or other plants.

From the far east to the far west of the prairies there is a gradual change, with the grass becoming shorter and the soil shallower and less fertile.

AN UNPREDICTABLE CLIMATE

People, animals, birds, and plants living on the prairies face a number of natural hazards caused by the climate.

Lack of water can be a serious problem in the prairies. Most of the rain and snow comes from moist air, which moves north from the Gulf of Mexico. Southeastern areas near the Gulf, such as Texas, get more rain than areas in the north and west, such as Saskatchewan in Canada. Most rain falls in the summer, between May and September, when temperatures are highest. Some of the rain evaporates

▶

Frosts are common on the prairies, but it is difficult to know when they will occur. They can kill young crops in spring and hinder harvesting in the autumn.

◀

These western prairies receive very little rain and have only short, dry grasses.

as soon as it falls and does not soak into the soil to become available for plants. Much of the rain also falls in thunderstorms and runs straight off the land into rivers.

However, the real problem is that the rain-bearing winds from the Gulf are unreliable, and the amount of rain that falls can vary greatly from year to year. This makes figures of average rainfall very deceptive. Records show that the prairies get a series of very dry years, such as the 1930s and 1950s, followed by a series of wet years, like the 1940s and 1960s.

When the prairies suffer from a series of very dry years, drought sets in. Streams and water holes dry up, plants die, and the landscape becomes brown. All the vegetation becomes tinder dry, and one spark from lightning can ignite it into a brushfire. Crops and animals cannot survive long under such

conditions and some farmers go bankrupt when a drought lasts for several years.

Winds can also cause problems, sweeping unchecked across the smooth, treeless plains. In summer the hot, dry winds parch the crops, which wither and die. In places where there is little ground cover of grass or crops, the wind can blow away the topsoil, whipping it into huge dust storms. Sometimes, in the colder months, air funnels down from the Arctic, bringing severe frosts. Late spring frosts can kill the young shoots of growing wheat, and early autumn frosts can make harvesting difficult.

The number of days in a year when frost or snow is present varies from roughly 265 in Canada to 125 in Texas. Snow generally lies on the prairies for five or six months, and temperatures can fall as low as −40°F.

When strong winter winds combine with heavy snow, blizzards sweep across the prairies. Blizzards last several days and whip the snow into huge drifts, blocking roads and closing airports.

During summer there are severe storms with thunder and lightning. Such storms are common throughout the prairies, and usually bring short downpours of heavy rain. Severe storms sometimes produce hailstones, some as big as golf balls. The impact of these hailstorms can be devastating, causing immense damage to crops.

In spring, dry air from the Pacific coast of North America crosses the barrier of the Rocky Mountains. As the air descends to the prairies it becomes even warmer and drier, bringing a sudden and spectacular rise in temperatures. While this air, known as the Chinook, is a welcome change from the winter cold, the sudden snowmelt can cause widespread flooding, especially in the west.

THE DELICATE BALANCE
The prairies have evolved over millions of years. About 20 million years ago, movements in the earth's crust threw up the huge mountains of the Rockies. At this time the

A Prairie Food Chain

Wolves and coyotes eat small animals

Buffalo and pronghorn antelope eat grass

Prairie dogs eat roots, berries

Mice eat roots, seeds and leaves

Bobolinks and other birds eat seeds or insects

Butterflies live in grass habitats

Falcons or owls eat other small birds and animals

Prairie dogs, on watch for predators, stand by their burrows.

prairies looked like a vast, grassy parkland broken by lots of trees. Animals similar to horses and antelopes grazed across these parklands and were hunted by wolves and bears.

Much later, about 500,000 years ago, enormous ice sheets started to advance and retreat across the prairies. They did this four times, across 70 percent of the area. Each time, the ice leveled the landscape, leaving behind deposits of sand, rocks, mud, and silt. When the ice sheets finally disappeared, about 20,000 years ago, there was no vegetation to hold the soil together. Winds blew the sand as far west as Nebraska, forming shifting sand dunes that are now called the Nebraska sandhills. The lighter silt and mud were blown east, where they were deposited as soft, round hills of fertile loess in Iowa and Nebraska. Both of these areas are part of the prairies.

In time, plants grew again on the prairie soils. These grasses, trees, and other plants have evolved over about 8,000 years. Now they form part of a very delicately balanced community that includes insects, birds, and animals, as well as the soil. This community is called an ecosystem. Within the ecosystem a distinctive set of insects feeds on prairie grasses and other plants. Butterflies such as the silverblue and the great spangled fritillary are a key part of this finely balanced prairie ecosystem. Birds such as the meadowlark feed on grass seeds or on insects. These birds may be eaten in turn by predatory birds such as the falcon.

The prairie ecosystem also supports a wide range of animals, including mice, whose sharp teeth can eat every part of the grass plant, from roots to leaves and seeds.

The prairie dog is the most famous local rodent. It is not a dog at all, but its call of alarm can sound like a dog barking. Prairie dogs dig elaborate underground burrows. Here they are safe from predators and are protected from winter cold and summer heat.

Before European settlers arrived, millions of buffalo grazed in huge herds across the prairies.

They often excavate their burrows to join up and form underground cities. One burrow discovered in the United States covered about 15,500 square miles and was home to millions of animals. Prairie dogs eat roots, seeds, and berries. Other prairie animals, such as the coyote and the fox, are predators and feed on prairie dogs or other small animals.

Animals that graze on grass, such as pronghorn antelope and buffalo (also called bison), were important elements of the prairie ecosystem. In the past, there were millions of buffalo, living in huge herds. They roamed across the grasslands in search of new shoots and leaves. Their droppings helped to fertilize the soil and improved conditions for grasses and other plants in the ecosystem. By eating grass shoots the buffalo and antelope stimulated the grass to grow young, strong shoots.

· THE · EARLY · INHABITANTS ·

The first settlers on the prairies were the Native Americans who were hunters and gatherers. It is estimated that they arrived more than 30,000 years ago by crossing a prehistoric land bridge from Asia to America. They lived a rather uncertain existence, because they ate only what they could find: fruits, berries, nuts, and roots. They supplemented this diet by occasionally killing buffalo for meat. In the early years, before the

▲
The Native Americans who lived on the prairies used horses to hunt buffalo, which provided their food, clothing, shelter, and weapons.

The buffalo was an important part of many Native American religious ceremonies.

horse was introduced to America, hunters had to chase the buffalo on foot, and they had only bows and arrows and axes, so many hunts ended without a kill. Sometimes massive kills of buffalo took place by driving herds over cliffs, then killing those still alive with spears and other weapons. The tribes moved across the prairies, following the migration of the buffalo.

Later, after 1600, the horse was introduced to Central America by the Spaniards. Gradually, horses spread to North America and their numbers soon increased. When herds of wild horses appeared on the prairies the Native Americans were quick to see their potential value. The horses were tamed so they could be ridden. This transformed the lives of tribes like the Cheyenne, Pawnee, and Sioux. They were able to pursue the buffalo across the prairies at high speed. People could travel many miles with far less effort. Many more buffalo could be killed so there was more food for the growing native population. The tribes soon developed new strategies for hunting in groups rather than as individuals. This process of cooperation made it possible to trap and kill many more buffalo than could be hunted by one person on his own. So successful were the original prairie tribes that other groups such as the Crow left the forests or mountains in search of a better life based on buffalo hunting.

Many Native Americans based their way of life entirely around the buffalo. The animals provided meat, and their fur was used for cloaks and warm, waterproof clothing. Buffalo hide was used to make tents. Buffalo bones were made into tools and weapons such as arrows and lances, and buffalo hide was used for shields. Buffalo teeth provided decorative necklaces, and the tribe's healer, or shaman, wore a headdress made from the animal's head. The buffalo was the symbol of wisdom and knowledge and was worshipped as a god.

Although the Native Americans were killing more buffalo than before, they still were not upsetting the delicate balance of the prairie ecosystem. There were so many millions of buffalo on the prairies that, even with the horse, the hunters made little difference to total numbers. Also, the Native Americans never killed more than they needed; they have always lived in harmony with their surroundings. Buffalo herds remained stable so the ecosystem remained intact.

CHANGING THE BALANCE

Life and the environment of the prairies began to change rapidly after 1830 in the United States and after 1870 in Canada, when settlers began to head west in search of new land. This was the "frontier," that is, the line of advancing farms and villages that pushed ever farther west.

The settlers viewed the prairies with dismay. It was a dry, grassy, and unfamiliar environment. To many it seemed like a desert, and the Americans of the 1840s and 1850s treated it as such. The only virtue of the prairies was that they were easy to cross on the way to the west coast.

The area had several problems for settlement by Europeans. First, it was largely treeless. People felt land that would not support trees was poor land. At that time, wood was the only fuel for the settlers' stoves. In addition, without trees there was no way of fencing the land or of building houses. The earliest attempts at building houses on the prairies were sod houses, which had walls of earth blocks, roofed with turf. Most of the

There were so few trees on the prairies that early settlers built their cabins out of earth blocks instead of timber.

prairie land was very dry and farmers from the east were not prepared for this. The varieties of wheat and corn crops that they had grown farther east were unsuited to such dry conditions, and their farming techniques were suited to wetter areas. The limited water supply was a further problem. Rivers flowed only during certain seasons, and water-holes were few and far between. The first settlers grabbed the land next to the water supplies; land away from water was considered largely valueless.

On the prairies of the U.S. settlers moving west came into sharp conflict with the Native American tribes. Time after time white settlers claimed the land, and tribes were forced to move away from their traditional hunting grounds. When the Native Americans objected they were met with force. As a result their resistance to the invasion of the newcomers became ferocious. The government's attempts to make land agreements with the Native Americans were overtaken by the speed of the settlers' move westward. Every time another tribe was forced to move, another war followed and eventually the tribe withdrew, broken, to a different region. Lands kept by the tribes, or set aside for them by the government, were later coveted by white settlers, who took them by force. In a continent with a long series of tragic wars between Native Americans and European settlers, the struggle was rarely as bitter as on the prairies.

One major area of disagreement was the use of buffalo as a resource. Settlers on their way west killed buffalo for food, but later, when railroads began to be laid across the prairies, buffalo slaughter began in earnest.

▲

Native Americans have often been portrayed as bloodthirsty by settlers. In fact, the opposite was often true.

The railroad companies hired hunters to shoot buffalo to feed their workers. Other hunters killed the buffalo for their hides, which could be sold for a good profit. Between 1850 and 1910 the buffalo population fell from 60 million to just a few hundred. White settlers had caused the total destruction of the Native Americans' traditional buffalo-hunting way of life.

The slaughter of the buffalo also began to change the delicate environmental balance of the prairies' ecosystem. With fewer buffalo the grass shoots were not eaten, so the grass did not grow as vigorously. The shorter grass produced less organic material so the soil

The coyote has been affected by changes in the prairie food chain. When the buffalo were killed off, the soil became less fertile. Plants did not grow as well, so fewer prairie dogs and other small animals could survive to provide food for coyotes.

became less fertile, particularly in the vital top layers. As the buffalo were killed there was less organic matter from their dung added to the soil. Soil fertility declined still further. Less fertile soils could not support the same range of prairie plants, such as orchids, as well as grasses, and some species of plants disappeared. The number of butterflies that fed on orchids was greatly reduced, and some varieties of butterfly almost certainly died out.

Such changes in the prairie habitat had important consequences for the insects, birds, and animals that depended on this ecosystem. For example, there was less food for the meadowlarks and other species that fed on seeds or on butterflies. In turn, there were fewer birds as prey for species like owls and falcons. Less fertile soils meant there was less food for prairie dogs. This affected the wolves and coyotes that preyed on the prairie dogs, because there was less for them to eat. The whole balance of the ecosystem began to change. The absence of the buffalo – a change in one part of the ecosystem – had a disastrous effect on other parts of the same system.

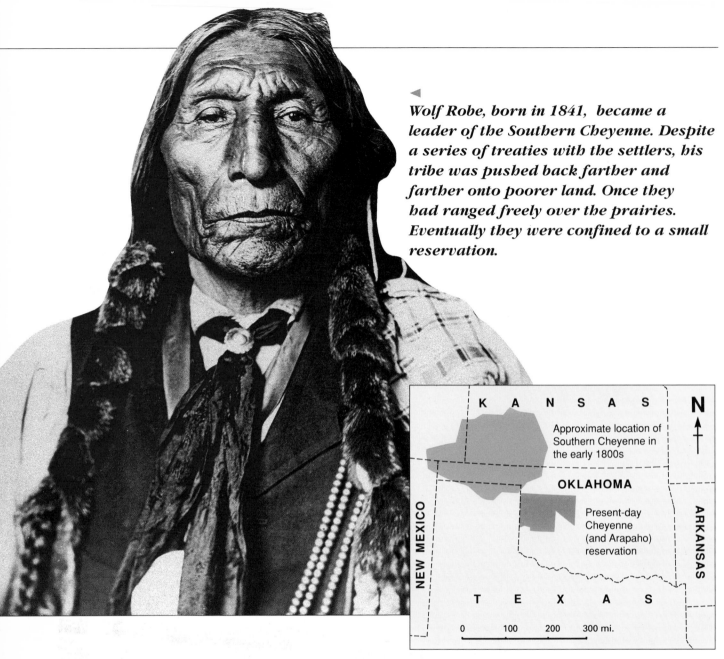

Wolf Robe, born in 1841, became a leader of the Southern Cheyenne. Despite a series of treaties with the settlers, his tribe was pushed back farther and farther onto poorer land. Once they had ranged freely over the prairies. Eventually they were confined to a small reservation.

K A N S A S

N

Approximate location of Southern Cheyenne in the early 1800s

OKLAHOMA

NEW MEXICO

Present-day Cheyenne (and Arapaho) reservation

ARKANSAS

T E X A S

0   100   200   300 mi.

CATTLE AND CROPS

Throughout the nineteenth century, Native Americans were driven from their traditional lands and turned into second-class citizens. Most settlers regarded them as savages who needed to be firmly contained, or even wiped out. They failed to see the wisdom of the Native Americans' traditional values, particularly those relating to the environment. Ultimately, the tribes suffered a series of military defeats which confined them to specific areas.

In theory, Native Americans have been treated differently in the U.S. and Canada. In Canada, in 1876, the Canadian Indian Act gave Native Americans the right to own land and freedom to practice their own religion and culture. In the U.S., treaties the Native Americans had signed with the government were taken back or ignored. But in both countries Native American communities have been confined to areas of poor land, called reserves in Canada and reservations in the

U.S. and in both countries Native Americans are generally still among the poorest people. Hundreds of years after European explorers first arrived in America, people such as the Innu in Canada still have not had their rights to their land recognized.

The reservations, or reserves in Canada, were usually the land that white settlers did not want. So some of the very driest parts of the prairies became Native American lands. Here, they were expected to change their entire life-style from buffalo hunting to farming instead. Instead of the bow and arrow and lance, they were forced to use the plow and the hoe.

Many efforts were made to teach European farming techniques to the Native Americans. However, the men regarded it as work more suitable for women, and few Native Americans had enough money to invest in the equipment needed. As a result, few of them became successful farmers.

This family of Native Americans was photographed in 1959, living in a state of extreme poverty. Many Native Americans are still among the poorest people in the U.S. and Canada.

As the Native Americans were driven from most of the prairies two new groups of white settlers – the ranchers and the farmers – claimed control over the grasslands. The ranchers arrived first. From 1860 to 1885 cattle ranching was the most profitable way of using a grassland area. At that time the prairies were useless to farmers, who lacked the tools and the expertise to cultivate them.

After many of the buffalo herds had been killed, cattle were driven north from Texas to feed the railroad workers. At the same time the population of the eastern U.S. and Canada was growing by more than 100,000 per year. More and more meat was wanted. The new railroads made it possible to carry live cattle back to the eastern towns for slaughter. As a result, cattle rearing began on a large scale on the prairies, from Alberta, Canada, in the north to Texas in the south. This was the time of the cowboy and the cattleman. Huge stretches of prairie became ranches and the cattle ran wild over unfenced land. The only

▲
Railways sped up development of the prairies. Towns and farms spread out along the railway lines, and cattle were transported back to provide meat for the eastern cities.

Ranches were too big to be fenced, and cattle ran wild over the grasslands. There were often arguments about who owned the cattle, sometimes causing fights between ranchers.

way for ranchers to tell which were their cattle was to burn brands into the animals' skin. Wells and streams provided water, and in the long, freezing winter the animals had to search for food on the open range.

Ranching began to change in the 1880s after the invention of refrigeration. It became possible to preserve meat by freezing it in refrigerated warehouses. America began to produce high-quality beef to sell in Europe. Better breeds of cattle such as the Hereford and Aberdeen Angus were imported to improve the quality of the herds. However, the new cattle were not very hardy and could not survive the cold winters. New cross-breeds of cattle were developed that could

▲

At first, farmers used horse-drawn plows for farming. Then, from the 1890s, steam-powered tractors were used for plowing and harvesting. However, the heavy machines started to compact the soil, causing problems with drainage.

survive in the harsh environment yet still give good meat. Ranchers also realized that they needed to provide some winter food for their animals rather than leave them out on the open range. So they grew hay, which was the main cattle food, together with root vegetables, such as turnips.

Farmers were only able to settle on the prairies as a result of a series of inventions that transformed their way of life. The steel plow made it possible to cut through the turf and cultivate the rich, stoneless soil. Barbed wire allowed farmers to fence off their fields and prevent cattle from eating their crops.

▲
This Canadian Pacific railroad company poster invited British people to buy its land and become farmers in Canada.

The new mechanical drills and harvesters made it easier to sow seed and harvest crops. Railroads pushed through the prairies linking the grain producers to markets in the east.

New types of wheat imported from Europe were another big improvement. These new varieties, such as Turkey red wheat, were hardier and quicker growing than older types. They could be planted in spring and harvested before the frosts of September.

During the nineteenth century farmers had also been spreading west. At first they farmed the more fertile, tallgrass prairies of the east. They grew wheat and corn and turned the prairies into grain fields. As the farmers advanced west the ranchers were pushed into drier, short-grass prairies where the pasture was poorer and droughts were more frequent. Farming was more profitable than ranching so in some cases farmers could buy out ranchers. In other cases the sheer numbers of farmers began to swamp the land and ranchers chose to move west where there was still open range. These changes were not always peaceful. Numerous range wars – between ranchers and farmers – raged before a pattern was established.

The governments of the U.S. and Canada encouraged immigrants to settle on these vast prairies. Both countries passed the Homestead Acts, which allowed any householder to claim 160 acres of land for a few dollars. Land could also be bought from railroad companies; land had been given to them by the government in exchange for building new railroads. The idea was that the railroad companies would encourage people to settle along their tracks in order to generate traffic for the railroad. The land was laid out in square miles and each farm was about half a mile square. The land began to take on a distinctive, checkerboard layout. Even today, roads and railroads run north to south or east to west. Very few roads cut diagonally across farmers' square fields.

· T H E · D U S T · B O W L ·

Many new settlers arrived in the prairie region from the wetter eastern parts of America in the 1880s and early 1900s. Farming the prairies was a new experience for them. They did not know that a series of wet years was normally followed by a series of dry years. They also failed to see the danger of plowing up the soil year after year. In the end the only way they could learn how to farm successfully was by trial and error, but the errors were very costly.

Steel plows had made it easier to cut through the dense surface layer of prairie turf. The plows had a moldboard that turned the sod over as the plow moved forward, exposing the soil to the weather. This meant that the soil dried out quickly, becoming dusty and easily blown away in high winds. This is soil erosion: the removal of the top layers of soil by wind or water. Also, growing wheat year after year on the same field soon exhausted the nutrients in the soil and crops failed.

After some years of drought, in the 1890s, farmers discovered that if a field was left uncultivated for a year, moisture would be stored in the upper layers of the soil, just below the surface. This would help to give a good yield for the next year's crop. But the soil surface had to be constantly broken up by raking the soil with a harrow. This kept the soil from developing wide cracks, so moisture stayed in instead of escaping through the cracks. Unfortunately, harrowing the soil merely added to the danger of soil erosion. By keeping a surface layer of dry, broken soil the farmers were creating an ideal environment for dust storms, causing severe erosion as wind blew away the most fertile topsoil.

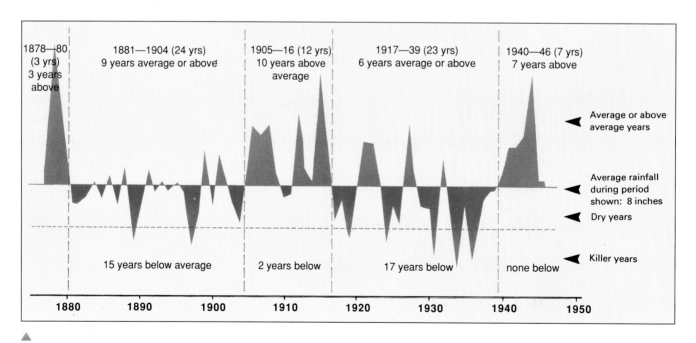

Rainfall on the prairies, 1878–1946.

Dust storms carried away topsoil and — as here in Oklahoma in 1936 — buried homes, sheds, and fences.

The dangers came to a head in the 1930s. These were years of drought. The summers were long and hot with only occasional rains. Snowfalls were below average so there was even less moisture than usual in the soil in spring. When the winds blew there was nothing to anchor the dried-out, powdery soil. The soil particles were swept high into the atmosphere and carried along for several thousand miles. There were many dust storms or "black blizzards," as they were called. They lasted for days and blotted out the sunlight, so that even at midday cars had to drive with their lights on. The choking dust blew into houses, under doors and around windows, and made breathing difficult. The winds piled up the soil in deep drifts against obstructions such as hedges or houses.

The worst problem for the farmers was that the most fertile soil was being blown away. In the 1930s it became common for fields in parts of the prairies to lose four inches of topsoil during a two-day storm. Topsoil contains the largest amount of organic material, which not only provides fertilizer for crops but also helps to conserve moisture in the soil and to hold it together. Once this layer was removed by erosion, only the underlying subsoil was left in which to grow crops. The subsoil contained far less organic matter and was far less fertile.

When the dust settled the topsoil had been blown away. Huge areas, from Saskatchewan, Canada, in the north to Texas in the south, were turned into desert. The whole area became known as the Dust Bowl. Thousands of farmers went bankrupt and were forced to abandon their farms and move to find work in towns and cities.

WHEAT FARMING

*W*heat has always been the main crop over the western parts of the prairies. In the north, in Canada and Dakota, winters are so cold that the wheat cannot be planted until spring. Then it has a growing season of only 90 days before it has to be harvested to beat the autumn frosts. Farther south, in Oklahoma and Texas, winters are much milder, so wheat is planted in the autumn, grows throughout winter and spring, and is harvested in late summer. Thus the crop has a much longer growing season than spring wheat and tends to give more reliable yields.

AGRIBUSINESS

Modern prairie farms are run as businesses, using the latest technology to get the maximum profit from the land. This type of farming is called agribusiness and has spread as farms have become bigger. Throughout the wheat-growing areas farms are large (over 2,500 acres) and are getting larger. The original farms were only 160 acres. However, it soon became apparent that farms needed to be much bigger in order to take advantage of the big tractors and farming machines that had been introduced. Large machines such as combine harvesters work most efficiently in

▶
To harvest a crop at the best time, several combine harvesters can use strong headlights and work all night, if necessary.

◀
Computers are now just as much a part of farming as tractors. Farmers must learn many skills and keep up with modern technology in order to make a living.

large fields. Big farms and big machines increase farm profits.

Another advantage of modern machinery is its speed. It can prepare land quickly so that seed can be planted without losing time. In the north, where the growing season is short, even the loss of a day can be serious. At harvest time, combine harvesters can take in the crop quickly, even working through the night with powerful headlights mounted on the machines.

Unfortunately, modern machines can damage the environment. The sheer size and weight of some of the trucks, combine harvesters, and tractors press down and compact the soil. Over the years, as the top-soil gets compacted, the air spaces in the soil become squeezed out. Soon water cannot get down through the soil and drainage becomes a serious problem. Waterlogging has caused problems on some prairie farms.

Similarly, big machines need big fields in which to operate. Prairie fields have become bigger and bigger over the years, but this has meant removing what few natural trees or hedges remained. Natural vegetation helps to protect the soil from winds, and the loss of these natural windbreaks has increased the rate of soil erosion. Their removal also destroys habitats for plants and animals.

Airplanes are a quick and efficient way of spraying pesticides over the huge prairie fields. Although pesticides get rid of insects that eat farmers' crops, they are also associated with eye and skin irritation or breathing difficulties among humans.

Most prairie farmers now grow several different crops and raise some beef cattle, as you can see from this patchwork of farmland in Kansas.

A wide range of chemicals is used on wheat farms. Selective weed killers can be used after the harvest to kill only the weeds and to leave the wheat stubble as protection against soil erosion. Other chemicals are used as fertilizers to increase yields, or as pesticides or fungicides to get rid of pests and diseases.

Such chemicals can create problems. For example, if too much nitrate fertilizer is used on the fields not all of it may be taken up by the plants. In this case, some nitrate may find its way into water supplies. Nitrate in drinking water has been linked to stomach cancer,

so farmers have been urged to limit their use of this fertilizer. Some fertilizers can also break down soil structure, making it more likely to blow away.

Other chemicals, used to kill insect pests, can also kill other harmless insects such as bees and butterflies. The use of pesticides is seen as one of the main reasons for the decline in the number of species of butterflies and other insects on the prairies.

People who live near fields that have been treated with chemicals often complain about health problems such as eye or skin irritation, or even difficulty in breathing. Such chemicals can be dangerous. The United States has taken action to ban some insecticides, such as DDT, which was shown to be harmful to health. DDT is particularly harmful because it can remain in an animal's body for a long time. When DDT-affected insects are eaten by an animal the DDT is passed on; when those animals are eaten, the DDT progresses higher up the food chain, becoming more and more concentrated with each step. In this way, the poisonous effects of DDT can reach many animals, and even find its way into human foods. Despite the harmful effects of such chemicals, many are still in widespread use.

New types of wheat that are resistant to diseases such as rust, a type of fungus, are constantly being introduced. Other types of wheat that are resistant to frost or drought have been developed, so wheat farms can operate in areas where the climate might have been a problem in the past. However, there is a problem of relying too much on just one crop. If the crop fails for any reason, such as drought, hailstorms, or insect pests, farmers might be ruined. Now wheat farmers might also raise some beef cattle.

Modern prairie farmers know they have the technical resources and government aid to rescue themselves if some sort of natural calamity arises. The dust-bowl years produced a generation of farmers who regarded the prairies' environment as being like a tiger. Now there is much greater confidence that the tiger has been tamed. As a result, areas that in the 1940s were regarded as too dry to plow are now cultivated. Millet is a new crop that can withstand drought. It is grown on farms in the drier areas and is a good cattle food.

Preventing Soil Erosion

Planting rows of trees to break the force of the wind.

Leaving the field covered with stubble or grass. This keeps the topsoil from being blown away, and also adds organic matter to the soil, which helps to bind it together.

Plowing along the line of the contours, rather than up and down the slope. This helps to keep loose soil in place, rather than letting it get washed down a hill by rain.

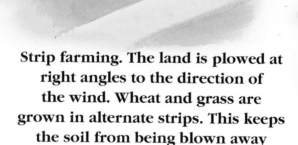

Strip farming. The land is plowed at right angles to the direction of the wind. Wheat and grass are grown in alternate strips. This keeps the soil from being blown away after the wheat has been harvested.

Building dams to store water for irrigation, which keeps the soil damp so that it is less likely to be blown away.

Prairie farmers learned about soil erosion the hard way. As a result they devised methods of farming to prevent soil erosion. These include the methods above.

As a result, soil erosion in the prairies has been greatly reduced, and some of the eroded areas have been reclaimed and planted with new, fast-growing grasses. The grasses bind the eroded soil, but the soil is too poor to support anything else, such as crops.

MAIZE FARMING

In the eastern part of the prairies, especially Iowa and Illinois, there is enough rain for corn to grow well. The hot summers ensure that the crops grow and ripen despite the relatively short growing season. Corn is the most reliable of the crops grown on the prairies. For many years this area was called part of the "corn belt," but it would be more correct to call it the "meat belt," since most of the corn is fed to cattle or pigs.

Farms in this area are mixed farms, growing a range of crops including corn and soybeans and also rearing pigs and cattle. Because corn is a demanding crop that takes many nutrients from the soil, it is often grown in rotation with alfalfa or hay to give the soil a chance to recover its fertility. Alfalfa is a legume and it helps to restore nitrogen to the soil. Soybeans are an important source of protein when made into vegetable oil and other foods. They also give a rich fodder crop for animals.

Three-quarters of the income of all farms in this part of the prairies comes from the sale of animal products. Pigs are the most common animal, followed by cattle brought in for fattening from the drier range lands to the west. Animal rearing is a much more profitable type of farming than simply selling the corn crop. It enables smaller farms to survive and still make a profit.

Modern pig farmers often keep the pigs indoors, in carefully controlled conditions, so that they grow as quickly as possible. This is called intensive farming.

Cattle remain important in the drier, western prairies, as on this midwestern farm.

RANCHING

Wheat and corn fields do not extend across the whole of the prairies to the Rocky Mountains. The western part of the prairies is too dry for successful crop growing. Here, the main form of land use is grazing. Beef cattle are reared and grazed on very big ranches. Because conditions are so dry, the grass is short and does not grow very quickly. Soils are shallow and not very fertile. So ranches have to cover several thousand acres in order to have enough grass to support sizeable cattle herds.

Despite the size of these large ranches the grass has been overgrazed in the past. This upset the delicate environmental balance: the grass disappeared and in some places was replaced by mesquite and sagebrush. These plants can resist drought more easily than grass, but are of little food value to cattle. Bare soil was exposed in some areas of Montana and Wyoming, and erosion followed.

The U.S. government has bought some of the eroded land, plowed it up, and planted it with fast-growing grasses. These new varieties of grasses can resist drought but still provide good food for cattle and horses. Unfortunately, this replanting is expensive so has only been carried out in a few parts of the western prairies.

·A·LARGE-SCALE· ·WATER·PROJECT·

A long-term solution to the problem of drought on the western prairies is the establishment of large-scale irrigation projects. These provide long-term storage of water in huge reservoirs, so that even in the driest years there should be sufficient water to irrigate both crops and pasture for cattle.

SOUTH SASKATCHEWAN RIVER PROJECT

In Canada, irrigation has been important since the 1900s, mainly in the provinces of Alberta and Saskatchewan. Rivers starting in the Rocky Mountains flow all year round, fed by melting snow in the mountainous upper reaches of the river system.

In Saskatchewan, in the central part of the prairies, a huge irrigation project has been completed. Saskatchewan was one of the areas worst hit by the drought of the 1930s, even though the Saskatchewan River was flowing through the area, fed by melting snow. However, it was not until 1958 that a decision was made to build dams along the river. It took from 1959 to 1967 to build the main dam. The dam wall is 3 miles long and filled with earth. Once it was completed a lake 140 miles long, called Lake Diefenbaker, filled up behind it. A second dam 2 miles long was also built to prevent this lake from spilling over into another valley.

The project irrigates land downstream from the dam as well as generating electricity. Along the shores of the lake recreation areas have been built to enable both locals and tourists to enjoy water sports thousands of miles from the sea.

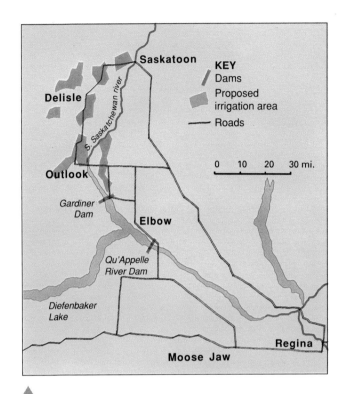

The South Saskatchewan River was dammed in two places to provide irrigation for huge areas of land.

The South Saskatchewan River Project has not been free of criticism. Farmers who lost land beneath the waters of Lake Diefenbaker claimed that the compensation they received from the government was inadequate. Another major difficulty was persuading wheat farmers to switch to crops like fruit and vegetables that are better able to use the irrigation water. Apart from the farmers' natural reluctance to change, the main drawback was the farmers' lack of knowledge about irrigated agriculture. They were not sure how much water to apply to the crops, when to apply it, and how to get rid of any surplus water that might remain. There were also doubts about how well the fruit trees would grow, what insect pests they might need protection against, and how local soils would suit them. Such farmers knew how their wheat fields had fit into the prairie ecosystem. They knew they had to apply artificial fertilizers and that they had to rotate their crops in order to conserve soil fertility. However, they were uncertain how this would change by switching to fruit or vegetable farming.

Irrigated farming has now become well established in this part of Saskatchewan. In general, most farmers are applying less artificial fertilizer than when they grew wheat. More trees, such as oak and willow, have been planted both as windbreaks and to regulate the water level in the soil. These trees have introduced more variety in the local habitat and so have encouraged a wide range of insects and birds to occupy the area.

This increase in the variety of habitat has to be offset against the loss of other habitats in the area flooded by the lake. Fields, marshes, and ditches were drowned by the rising waters of the lake. Insects, reptiles (such as frogs, toads, and newts), and small animals (such as mice) were forced to move,

▶

A crop in the central U.S., irrigated by water from the Ogalala aquifer, a natural underground reservoir.

◀

A satellite photograph taken from above the South Saskatchewan River, where it passes through the Canadian province of Alberta before the water flows into Lake Diefenbaker. It shows the grid pattern of large fields and the green areas of irrigated land.

or in some cases died out when their habitat was destroyed.

However, there are other environmental problems. Some of the irrigation water dissolves mineral salts from the soil as it soaks downward. In the hot summers some of this water is drawn back up to the surface as the water in the topsoil evaporates. As the water rises and evaporates, it deposits the mineral salts in the surface layers of the soil. These salts are toxic to many plants. They can be removed only by installing good field drains and then flushing more irrigation water through the soil to carry the salts away.

UNDERGROUND WATER

Some farmers can irrigate from natural water sources. Lying under the prairies, from Nebraska to Texas, is a huge underground reservoir known as the Ogalala aquifer. It is named after the Sioux tribe that lives in part of the area. The aquifer is a major source of water for irrigation, but it is rapidly being used up.

THE ENERGY INDUSTRY

Traditionally, the prairies have been an agricultural rather than an industrial area. The main types of industry that grew up before 1947 were all connected with agriculture. Towns were centers for flour milling or the provision and repair of agricultural machinery. The situation began to change after 1947 when vast deposits of oil were discovered in Alberta, Canada. The Leduc oil field was developed near Edmonton, which grew from being a medium-sized town serving part of Alberta into a large city. To the south, Calgary also began to grow. The discovery of oil and natural gas enabled Alberta to become one of the wealthiest states in Canada.

Alberta also has the world's largest reserves of oil sands. These sands contain huge amounts of oil but so far have not been widely developed. The main problem is the expense of separating the oil from the sand. At present, the sands represent a valuable energy reserve for Canada, which may be developed in the future if the world oil price rises significantly.

A set of major oil and gas pipelines has been built from Alberta, west across the Rocky Mountains to British Columbia, Canada, and Washington State. Another set of pipelines runs east to Lake Superior and the industrial cities around the Great Lakes. There are also large deposits of oil and gas in Kansas, Oklahoma, and Texas. The energy from prairie oil is used in wide areas of both the United States and Canada.

Huge new oil refineries, like this one at Edmonton in Canada, are needed to process the oil that has been discovered under the prairies before it can be used.

Oil brings jobs and money to the prairies, but drilling scars the landscape and causes pollution.

The growth of the oil industry has not been without problems. Despite the precautions taken oil spills have polluted rivers and water supplies near Edmonton and Calgary in 1979 and again in 1990. Drilling for oil and gas on a large scale has led to environmental damage: land has been polluted by oil and by the numerous chemicals and muds used in the drilling process. In some cases, roads have been carved through formerly productive farmland. Abandoned drilling rigs continue to represent potential threats to the environment if chemicals left on the sites escape into the air or water. Oil pipelines cut across fields, streams, roads, and railroads. The safety record of these pipelines is good, but any break would lead to massive pollu-

tion of the surrounding area and a serious loss of wildlife.

As well as oil and gas resources in the U.S., there are major deposits of coal in Wyoming, Montana, and North Dakota. Mining and transporting coal also cause pollution.

Oil, gas, and coal are nonrenewable resources. Once they have been used they are gone forever. Thus the oil fields and coal mines of the prairies will eventually run out. So far, scientists have been unable to find enough cheap, acceptable replacements for many energy needs, from fueling power plants to running private cars. Until such alternatives become available, large-scale extraction of oil, gas, and coal will continue on the prairies.

▲

A potash mine. Potash is a useful fertilizer, but digging it out creates huge holes in the ground, and the heavy mining machinery causes pollution.

POTASH MINING

In Saskatchewan, deposits of potash have been found. Potash is an important soil fertilizer, vital to the continued development of wheat and corn farming on the prairies. The potash was discovered by accident during exploration for oil. However, further exploration confirmed the existence of a broad belt of potash beneath the soils of Saskatchewan. The potash was formed millions of years ago when it was the bed of an ancient lake. When the lake dried up it left behind a vast deposit of potash. Mining the potash is not easy. Most mines date from the 1960s, but new equipment has been introduced to maintain output. Because the soils of Saskatchewan need little potash, most of the mines' output is sold to farms in the U.S.

Potash mining can damage the environment. Huge holes have been carved out of the ground where the potash is close to the surface. Where potash is mined from underground, the land above has often collapsed, leaving great hollows that usually fill with water. As more and more potash is extracted from underground, so the surface hollows have grown. Once the potash has been mined it is crushed and concentrated. The processing plants pollute the air of surrounding areas with dust and fumes.

SERVICE AND HIGH TECH INDUSTRY

In addition to the development of extractive industries like oil, gas, and potash, modern service industries have expanded rapidly in the prairie towns of the U.S. and Canada. As people flocked to the prairies to find work in the expanding mining and oil towns, so industries such as banking, insurance, and finance also expanded to service the growing population. The attractions of the wide open prairie environment with its fresh air and closeness to the scenic Rocky Mountains helped to encourage workers to move to prairie cities like Denver and Calgary.

Some modern high tech industries linked to computer manufacture have also opted for locations in the center of the North American continent that are connected to the rest of the United States and Canada by good roads, railroads, and air routes.

▲
The skyscrapers of Calgary are paid for with the profits from oil and wheat, plus newer industries such as banking, insurance, and computers.

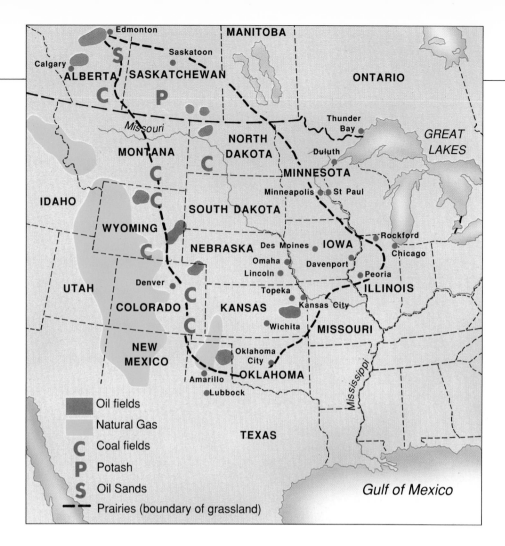

Mineral, oil, gas, and coal deposits are scattered throughout the prairies. These, and the newer service industries, have led more and more people to move there to work, and large cities have begun to appear.

POPULATION ON THE MOVE

The population of the prairies continued to grow up to 1930. Most of these people settled on homesteads, obtained from the government for a low price. Life for the farmers and their families could be very lonely, as the prairies were vast and the nearest neighbor could be 20 miles away. Due to the distances and limited transportation, people did not travel away from their farms very often.

Today, however, life-styles on the prairies are very different, and all the changes have had an impact on the environment. Cars and trucks have made travel easier and faster, enabling farmers and their families to move around more. Intensive farming has led to greater use of machinery such as trucks, tractors, and combine harvesters. Intensive

methods and increasing farm sizes also mean that fewer people are needed to work on the farms, and so more people work in towns and cities. The population of cities has increased as many people have moved away from the country in order to work in service industries or in manufacturing. Rail and air services, as well as roads, link the prairies' major towns and cities.

All this increased use of vehicles and machinery, and the move toward urbanization, have contributed to further environmental pollution. Unfortunately, some people who live on the prairies take their surroundings for granted and assume that pollution and destruction of resources are not serious problems that will affect them in the future.

· T H E · F U T U R E ·

The prairies have experienced enormous change in the last 150 years. Hardly any of the original "natural" prairie environment remains. Virtually all of it has been changed by human actions, especially by farming. The tallgrass prairies have been virtually replaced by fields of wheat and corn. The original ecosystem with its close links between soil, plants, insects, birds, and animals has been radically altered. Chemicals are needed to improve soil fertility and to kill insect pests. However, such chemicals have failed to maintain the best elements of soil structure, especially its ability to hold water. Chemicals have also destroyed wildlife and led to the loss of species. Water supplies have been polluted and habitats destroyed.

The basic problem is that the present system of prairie farming is not environmentally sustainable. That is, it cannot continue without damaging the environment. The challenge is to find a system that is environmentally sustainable and that still allows crops to be produced in large quantities. This is important because the prairies are vital to the rest of the world as a supplier of wheat and corn. Some grain goes as aid to developing countries, and some enters world trade and is sold to countries such as Russia. In addition, the prairies will continue to be the "bread-basket" of both Canada and the U.S. So, given that farming must and will continue to be vital on the prairies, can it be made environmentally sustainable?

The widespread use of chemicals is damaging to the environment. In future, farmers may be able to use more methods of biological control – such as pest-eating insects – instead of chemical pesticides.

One main hope lies in persuading farmers to adopt less environmentally damaging methods. Using chemicals less often would help. Farmers would save money by not having to buy as many chemicals, and although there would be slightly lower yields and more damage from pests, some farmers would be better off. The increased use of animal manure instead of chemical fertilizer would improve soil structure as well as fertility. Some biological controls for pests and diseases are now available. These use insects, higher up in the food chain, that feed on insect pests that damage crops. Again, this can increase crop yields without destroying other beneficial insect species. Such biological solutions are not available for every pest and disease problem, but research continues to find further environmentally friendly controls.

As well as the changes in farming methods there are attempts to revive some of the original prairie grasslands. The aim is to show how some areas of land can be restored to biological diversity and flourish alongside the farming environment.

▲
Animal manure can be used for fertilizer instead of man-made chemicals.

Restoring the Prairies' Balance

Birds of prey are attracted by small birds and animals

Insects such as butterflies, bees and wasps are attracted to plants

Foxes and coyotes eat smaller animals

Grasses add organic material, and chemicals like antibiotics

Birds are attracted by plants and insects

Plant grasses

Orchids and other flowers flourish

RESTORING A PRAIRIE ENVIRONMENT

At Northbrook and Batana near Chicago, Illinois, attempts are being made to resurrect the natural prairie environment. Areas have been cleared by fire and then seeds of the original grasses planted on prepared sites. Within two years these experimental plots had a rich ecosystem of grasses, orchids, and insects, which in turn led to the return of species like the eastern bluebird, long absent from the region. Other species such as meadowlarks, bobolinks, falcons, coyotes, and foxes have also been attracted back to these new prairies as food chains have been re-established. The aim of this type of restoration is both to halt further damage to the present prairie system, and recreate something similar to the original system that will have to survive alongside the farmlands.

One important discovery made in these trials is that re-establishing the original prairie environment involves starting with certain key plants, particularly bluestem grass and Indian grass. These prepare the way for other plants by adding antibiotic chemicals to the soil. These kill off some plant species and encourage others. The increase in organic material from the grasses in turn feeds a series of flowering plants. It seems that prairies return to their original condition by steps, over years or even decades. Until then people have to tend the system, cutting back the invading species and planting the desired ones. If this is not done, invading weeds take over and form a thick mat on the soil surface. This keeps prairie species from becoming established and slows down the process of returning to the original environment. Eventually, it is hoped, people will be able to leave the cleansing process to fire, and in a few patches to grazing animals like the buffalo. However, so few buffalo now survive, mostly in protected parts of national parks, that some form of human management of the natural prairies seems likely to continue for the foreseeable future.

On the prairies, farms are large and getting larger. They use more expensive machinery than ever before and employ fewer people. Farming has become less of a traditional way of life and more a business. Many prairie farms are now owned by large companies such as supermarket chains and meat packing firms. Despite this, it is still possible to find family farms that date from early homesteader times.

There are now about three million Native Americans in Canada and the U.S. Their lands cover 5 million acres of land in Canada and 86 million acres in the U.S. Traditional ways of life and culture have survived in most of these communities. There are schools, clinics, and even hospitals on some tribal lands. Some Native American people are determined to preserve their remaining land. They have banded together to promote their people's rights and to keep their culture alive.

◀
Native Americans – the original prairie-dwellers – still meet to celebrate their culture, as here at a pow-wow at Pine Ridge in South Dakota.

The kind of prairie this young girl will see when she grows up — whether a monotonous landscape or a rich, varied environment — will depend on choices that are being made now about how the prairies should be used.

Some of the Native Americans are farmers who manage to raise crops of corn on some of the poorest prairie land. Others rear cattle. These people retain an awareness of the fragility of the prairie ecosystem, but their lands are often poor quality. Native Americans are among the poorest people in North America, so they often lack the money to develop their lands as they would like.

The prairies look set to become less dependent on farming. The development of the oil and gas industries in the prairie region has led to the construction of new chemical factories, making everything from paints and plastics to pharmaceuticals. Potash mining is important, as are the new high tech industries such as computers, electronics, and telecommunications. The difficulty in the future will be balancing the environmental damage that such industries can cause against the economic benefits they bring. Attempts are being made to clean up the industries and reduce their impact on the environment. This is expensive and time consuming and often takes second place to job creation.

The only real future for the prairies is one in which farming, industry, and the environment can coexist in harmony. The key is sustainable development: whatever changes take place in farming, mining, industry, and towns on the prairies in the future must not threaten the environment on which everything else depends. Unless the lessons of past mistakes are learned and used to guide future developments, further mistakes could do more harm to an already degraded environment.

GLOSSARY

Agribusiness Modern intensive farming that uses chemicals and machines to increase output and profit.

Conserve Protect from harm or loss, for the future.

Crop rotation Regularly changing the crops grown on a field to keep the soil fertile.

Drought A long period with little rainfall, causing a water shortage.

Ecology The study of life forms in their natural environment and the relationships between them.

Ecosystem A community of plants, animals, insects and other organisms and the environment in which they live and react to each other.

Endangered species Types of plants, animals, insects, or reptiles that are in danger of becoming extinct.

Fertility The level of plant nutrients (food) in the soil.

Habitat An environment that provides a home for insects, plants, birds, and animals.

High tech industries Industries that use the most up-to-date equipment to produce goods or services. Also industries that produce high-tech goods such as computers.

Intensive farming A type of agriculture that depends on large inputs of expensive fertilizer, food, and machinery to get high yields.

Irrigation Watering the land to help crops grow.

Loess A type of moist or moldy soil or clay.

Mixed farming Agriculture in which farmers rear both crops and animals.

Nitrates Chemicals used in fertilizers.

Overgrazing Keeping too many animals on one area so that the grass is eaten away before it has a chance to grow again.

Pesticides Chemicals used to kill insect pests.

Pollution The presence in the environment of harmful substances, such as smoke from factories or dangerous chemical waste.

Semiarid Places with an annual rainfall of 10-23 inches.

Soil erosion Removal of topsoil by wind or water.

Species A group of living things that are alike and can breed with each other.

Tribe A group of families who live and work together, and are perhaps related to each other by a common ancestor.

Urbanization The change of country to town or city, and the expansion of towns or cities into the countryside.

Yield The amount of grain produced by a crop or the output produced per acre of land.

· B O O K S T O R E A D ·

Campbell, Maria. *People of the Buffalo: How the Plains Indians Lived.* Buffalo, NY: Firefly Books Ltd., 1992.

Chrisp, Peter. *The Farmer Through History.* Journey Through History. New York: Thomson Learning, 1993.

Kerrod, Robin. *Food Resources.* The World's Resources. New York: Thomson Learning, 1994.

Landau, Elaine. *Cowboys..* First Books. New York: Franklin Watts, 1989.

Landau, Elaine. *The Sioux..* First Books. New York: Franklin Watts, 1989.

McCall, Edith. *Pioneering on the Plains.* Frontiers of America. Chicago: Childrens Press, 1980.

Myers, Arthur. *The Cheyenne.* First Books. New York: Franklin Watts, 1992.

Reed-King, Susan. *Food and Farming.* Young Geographer. New York: Thomson Learning, 1993.

Siy, Alexandra. *Native Grasslands.* New York: Macmillan Children's Group, 1991.

Stone, L. *Prairies.* Vero Beach, FL: Rourke Corp., 1989.

· U S E F U L A D D R E S S E S ·

Agriculture Council of America
1250 I Street NW, Suite 601
Washington, DC. 20005

American Indian Heritage Foundation
6051 Arlington Blvd.
Falls Church, VA 22044

Department of Agriculture
14 Independence Avenue SW
Washington DC. 20250

Environmental Protection Agency
401 M Street SW
Washington, DC. 20460

Friends of the Earth (U.S.A.)
218 D Street SE
Washington, DC 20003

Indian Heritage Council
Henry Street
Box 2302
Morristown, TN 37816

Native American Community Board
P. O. Box 572
Lake Andes, SD 57356-0572

The Nature Conservancy
1815 Lynn Street
Arlington, VA 22209

Prairie Club
940 Lee Street, Suite 204
Des Plaines, IA 60016

Sierra Club
730 Polk Street
San Francisco, CA 94109

United States Committee for the United Nations Environment Program
2013 Q Street NW
Washington DC 20009

I N D E X

Numbers in **bold** refer to pictures as well as text